THAT'S STRANGE!

THE GHOST SHIP MARY CELESTE

Tom Jackson

Lerner Publications ◆ Minneapolis

Copyright © 2025 by Lerner Publishing Group, Inc.

All rights reserved. International copyright secured. No part of this book may be reproduced, stored in a retrieval system, or transmitted in any form or by any means—electronic, mechanical, photocopying, recording, or otherwise—without the prior written permission of Lerner Publishing Group, Inc., except for the inclusion of brief quotations in an acknowledged review.

Lerner Publications Company
An imprint of Lerner Publishing Group, Inc.
241 First Avenue North
Minneapolis, MN 55401 USA

For reading levels and more information, look up this title at www.lernerbooks.com.

Main body text set in ITC Franklin Gothic.
Typeface provided by International Typeface Corporation.

Library of Congress Cataloging-in-Publication Data

Names: Jackson, Tom, 1972– author.
Title: The Ghost Ship *Mary Celeste* / Tom Jackson.
Description: Minneapolis : Lerner Publications, 2025. | Series: UpDog books. That's strange! | Includes bibliographical references and index. | Audience: Ages 8–11 | Audience: Grades 4–6 | Summary: "The Mary Celeste was found abandoned with all items still on board. Why did the crew leave the ship so fast? Curious readers explore the details of the ship's failed voyage" — Provided by publisher.
Identifiers: LCCN 2024015123 (print) | LCCN 2024015124 (ebook) | ISBN 9798765648193 (library binding) | ISBN 9798765662533 (paperback) | ISBN 9798765658956 (epub)
Subjects: LCSH: Mary Celeste (Brig)—Juvenile literature. | Disappearances (Parapsychology) —Juvenile literature.
Classification: LCC G530.M37 J34 2025 (print) | LCC G530.M37 (ebook) | DDC 910.9163 —dc23/eng/20240408

LC record available at https://lccn.loc.gov/2024015123
LC ebook record available at https://lccn.loc.gov/2024015124

Manufactured in the United States of America

1 – CG – 12/15/24

Table of Contents

A Ship With No Crew   4

Follow the Facts   10

Explaining the Mystery   20

What Really Happened?   26

Glossary   30

Check It Out!   31

Index   32

A Ship With No Crew

In 1872, a ship was found in the Atlantic Ocean. It was 400 miles (650 km) from land.

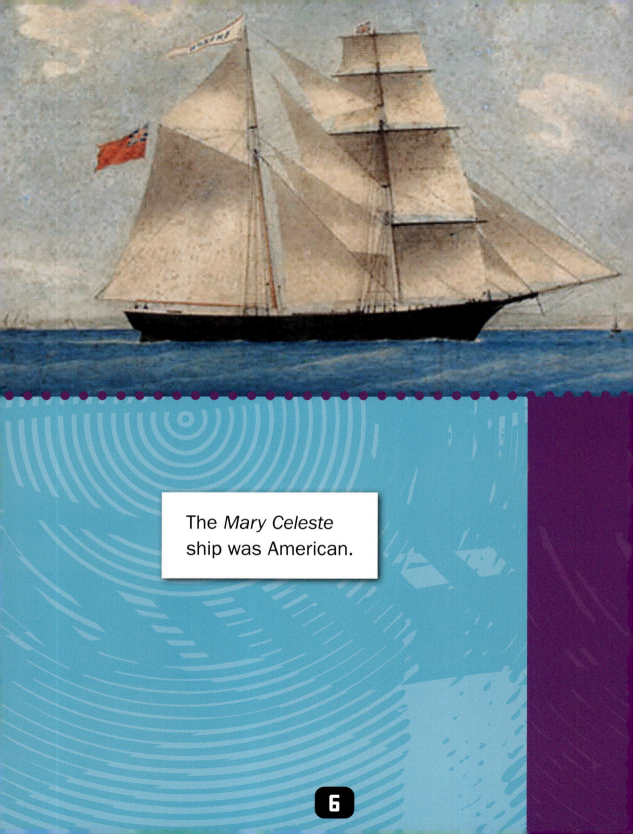

The *Mary Celeste* ship was American.

There was no one on board.

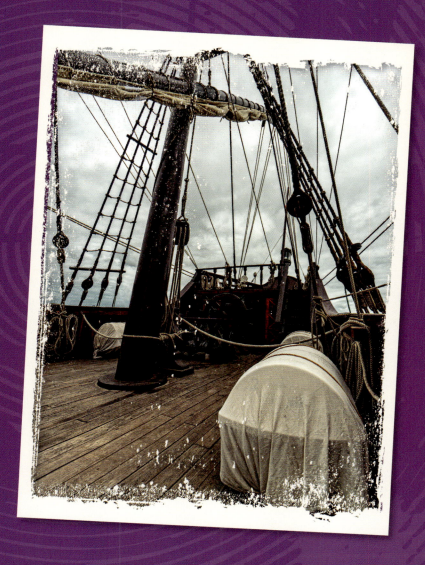

The crew's things were still in the cabins.

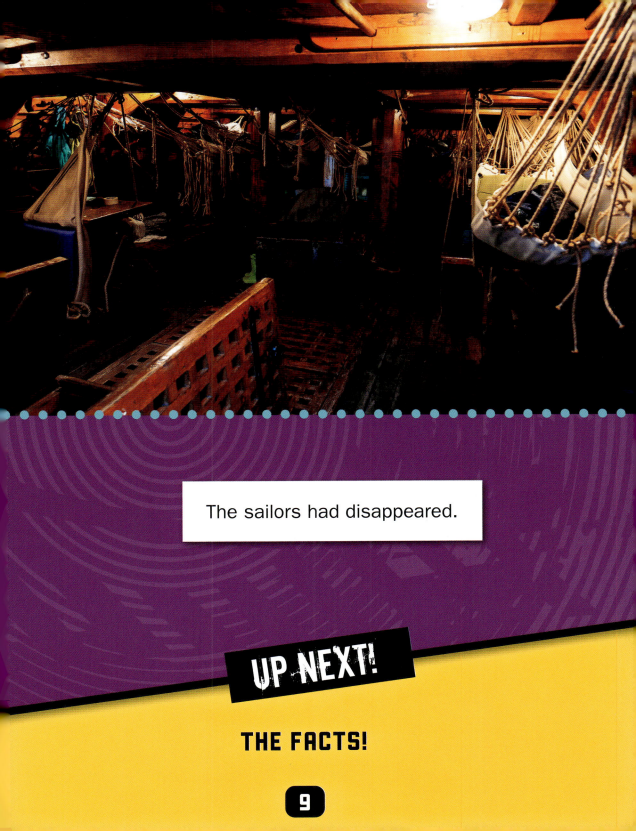

The sailors had disappeared.

UP NEXT!

THE FACTS!

Follow the Facts

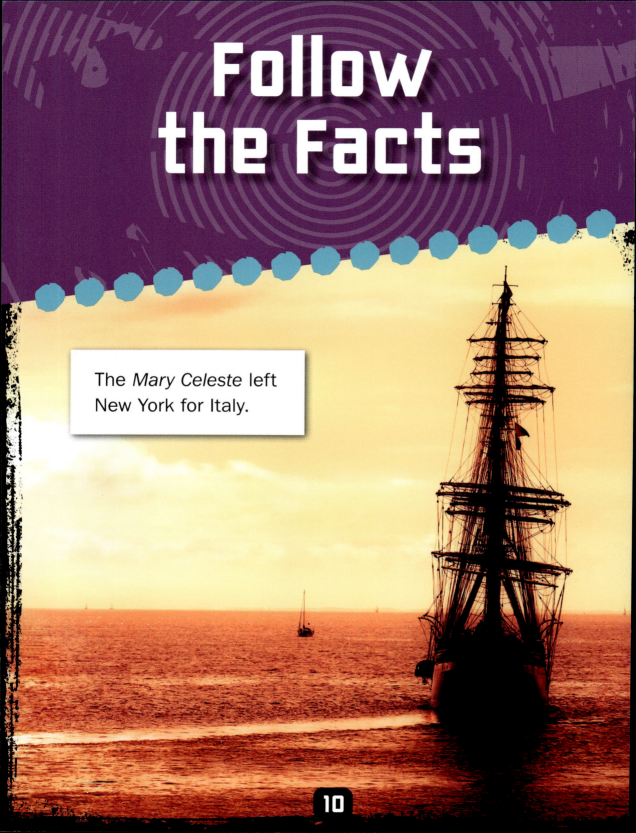

The *Mary Celeste* left New York for Italy.

The ship never arrived.

There was water in the bottom of the ship.

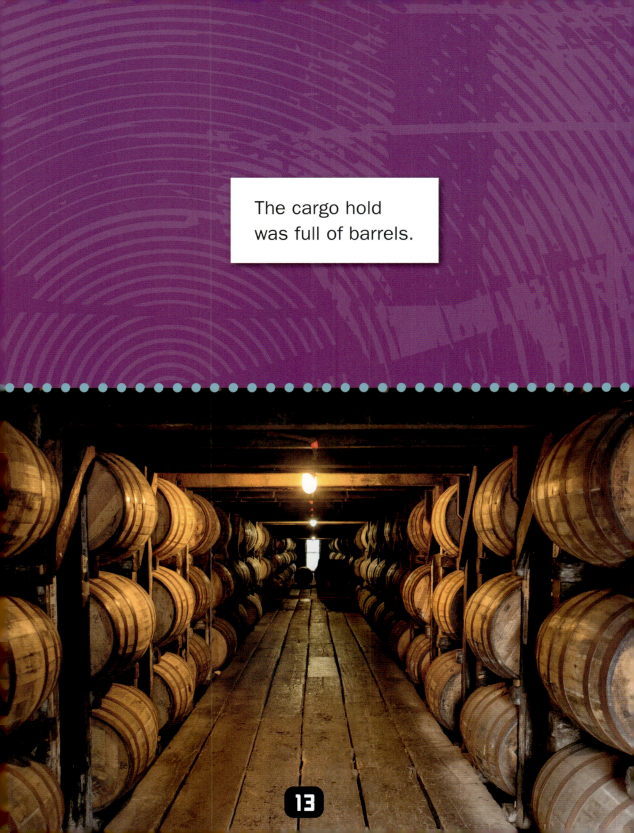

The cargo hold was full of barrels.

The *Mary Celeste* was not sinking. It had food and water on board.

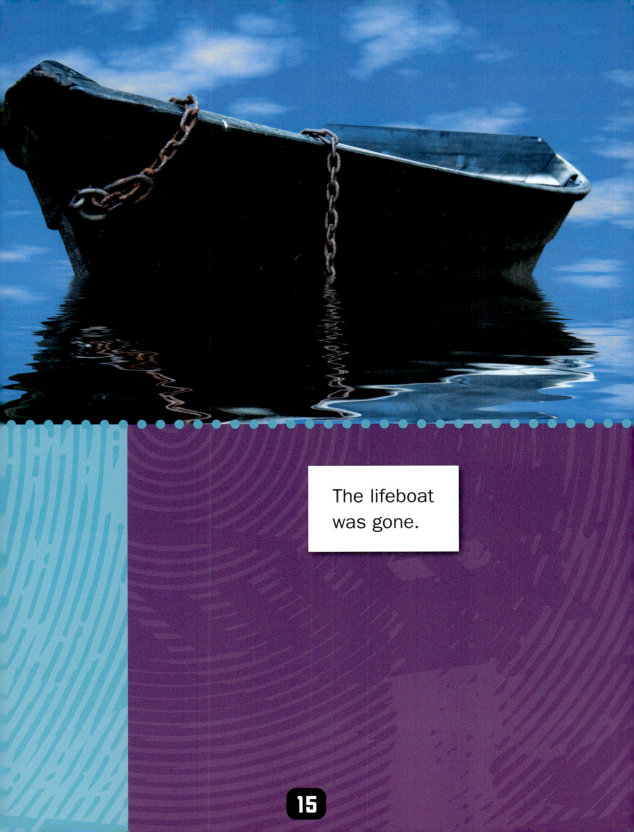

The lifeboat was gone.

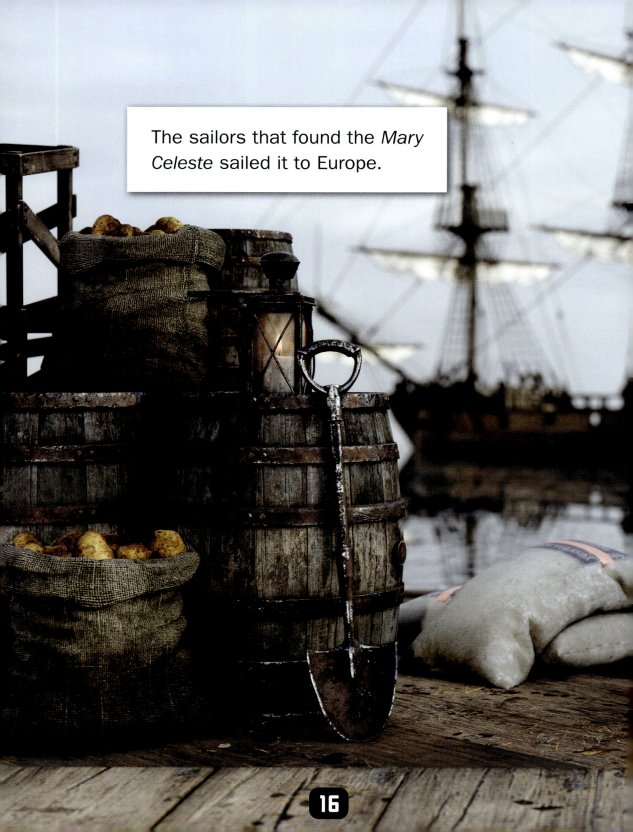

The sailors that found the *Mary Celeste* sailed it to Europe.

List Break!

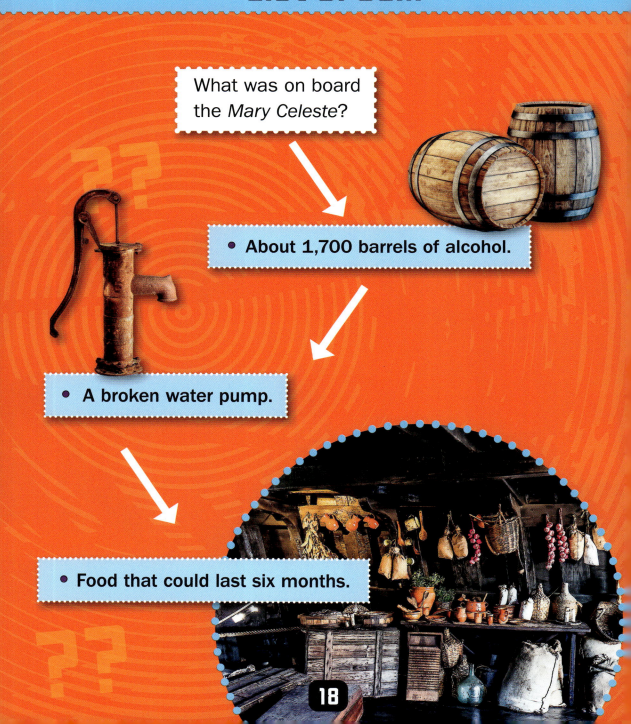

What was on board the *Mary Celeste*?

- About 1,700 barrels of alcohol.
- A broken water pump.
- Food that could last six months.

Other famous ghost ships:

OCTAVIUS (1775)
The crew were all frozen. The captain was still sitting at his desk.

BAYCHIMO (1931)
Got stuck in ice and drifted around empty for 38 years.

RYOU-UN MARU (2012)
Washed away by a tsunami in Japan. It was found one year later near Canada.

Explaining the Mystery

People wondered what happened on the *Mary Celeste*.

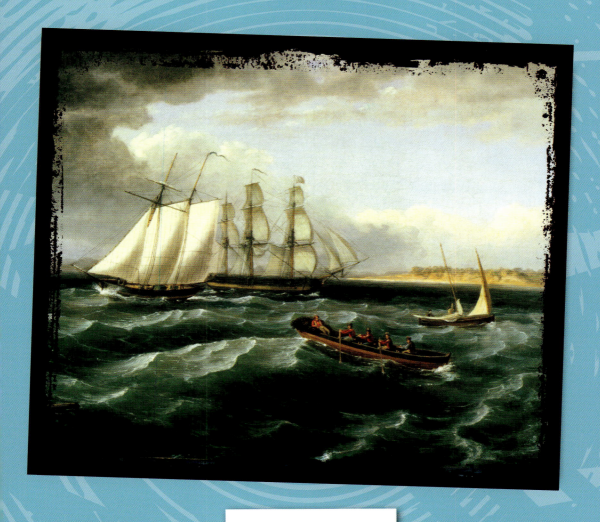

Were the crew chased away by someone?

Some of the alcohol barrels were leaking.

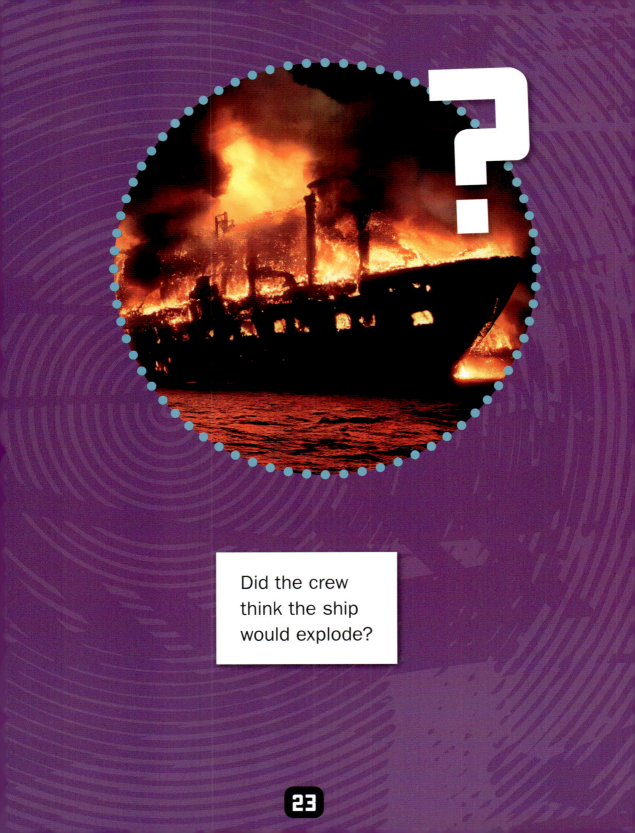

Did the crew think the ship would explode?

The pirate flag

Maybe the sailors that found the *Mary Celeste* were pirates.

Did they kill the crew and lie?

UP NEXT!

THE MOST LIKELY STORY.

What Really Happened?

People think the captain got lost.

The ship was filling with water. He thought the *Mary Celeste* would sink.

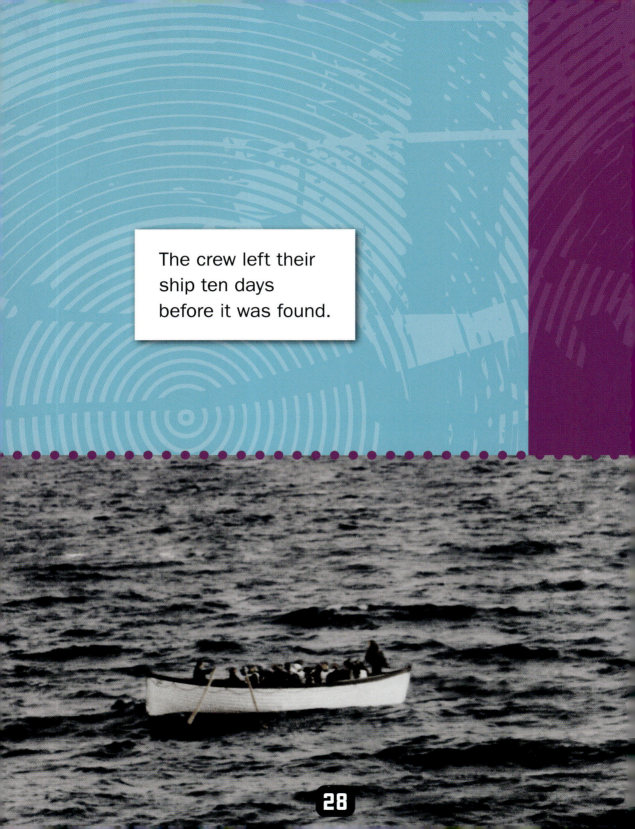

The crew left their ship ten days before it was found.

Their lifeboat probably sunk in a storm.

Glossary

alcohol: a liquid chemical that burns easily

cargo: the items being carried by a ship

lifeboat: a small escape boat used by a crew when their ship becomes unsafe

pirate: a sailor that attacks other ships and takes them over

tsunami: a very large wave caused by an earthquake under the sea

Check It Out!

Academic Kids: Mary Celeste
https://academickids.com/encyclopedia/index.php/Mary_Celeste

Bell, Samantha. *12 Suspenseful Mysteries*. Mankato, MN: 12 Story Library, 2020.

Britannica Kids: Famous Ships
https://kids.britannica.com/students/article/famous-ships/277035

Kiddle: Mary Celeste Facts for Kids
https://kids.kiddle.co/Mary_Celeste

Loh-Hagan, Virginia. *Mary Celeste*. Ann Arbor, MI: Cherry Lake Publishing, 2018.

Ziemann, Kimberly. *The Mary Celeste*. Mendota Heights, MN: Apex, 2023.

Atlantic Ocean, 4

cabins, 8
captain, 19, 26
cargo, 13

food, 14

ghost ships, 19

lifeboat, 15, 29

New York, 10

pirates, 24

sailors, 9, 16, 24

Photo Acknowledgments

Image credits: Oxanaso/Shutterstock, pp. 3, 23; muratart/Shutterstock, pp. 4–5; Slate magazine/Wikimedia Commons, p. 6; ENRIQUE ALAEZ PEREZ/Shutterstock, pp. 7, 9; DMITRII SIMAKOV/Shutterstock, p. 8; Rangpl/Dreamstime.com, p. 10; THPStock/Dreamstime.com, p. 11; SEALANDSKYPHOTO/Shutterstock, p. 12; Kelly vanDellen/Shutterstock, p. 13; Matt Sheppard/ Shutterstock, p. 14; Tund/Shutterstock, p. 15; Digital Storm/Shutterstock, pp. 16–17; AlexRoz/Shutterstock, p. 18 (top); Juan Nel/Shutterstock, p. 18 (bottom); animix/Shutterstock, p. 19 (top); Natallia Yaumenenka/Dreamstime.com, p. 19 (bottom); Aastels/Shutterstock, p. 20; The White House Historical Association/Wikimedia Commons, p. 21; Dimbar76/Dreamstime.com, p. 22; donfiore/Shutterstock, p. 24; Dino Osmic/Shutterstock, p. 25; U.P.images_photo/Shutterstock, p. 26; T-Design/Shutterstock, p. 27; Everett Collection/Shutterstock, p. 28; Yoo1122/Shutterstock, p. 29. Design elements: sokolovski/Shutterstock, pp. 1–32.

Cover: sokolovski/Shutterstock; Slate magazine/Wikimedia Commons; Natykach Nataliia/Shutterstock.